The MRS. Ministry

Making The Most of YOUR Ministry as a Woman and as a Child of God.

by Cathy L. Corle

copyright 2004
Revival Fires! Publishing
ISBN 1-932744-19-3
printed in the United States of America

Dear Friend,

I'm excited that you're about to let me share with you some of my thoughts and ideas and the lessons that the Lord has been teaching me lately.

It has long been my belief that most Christian ladies have no understanding of how very important they are, not only in the eyes of God, but also to all those who know them. The devil often discourages us by making us believe that we are unimportant and unnoticed. He will also twist this idea to tempt us, trying to convince us that our part is not that important anyway, so it won't do any damage to leave it undone, or to totally walk away from God's will for our lives.

God has an important and eternal purpose for every one of us, a ministry for us to carry out. Though we may think that no one in the world notices, God is watching. Do we love Him enough to do what He wants us to do? Someday we will stand before Him to face our reward or loss of reward, and then we will fully realize the importance of the work that God has given us to do. But if you never realize it before then, it will be much too late.

I'd like to remind you of this idea as it relates to our relationship to the Lord, to our husbands, to our children, to our local church, and to the world around us. I pray that this little 'heart to heart talk' we're about to have within the pages of this book will be just the encouragement you've been needing.

Because of Jesus,
Cathy Corle
Luke 1:38

Making the Most of Your Ministry

Chapter One

"...Take heed to the ministry which thou hast received in the Lord, that thou fulfil it."
(Colossians 4:17)

We all have times of re-evaluating and rededicating or at least we should, and the beginning of a brand new year always seems like a good time to schedule such a meeting with yourself and the Lord. Much of the preaching and teaching that we hear does not consist of ideas that are new to us, but rather a repetition of what we've already learned (and maybe forgotten). That's just part of our human nature, and it's as universal as 'all have sinned'.

Often in the Bible we see statements like the one the Apostle Paul made in II Timothy 1:6: *"Wherefore I put thee in remembrance..."* or in verse 14 of chapter two: *"Of these things put them in remembrance..."* We have a constant need to be reminded of the most important things in our lives, and the more important the topic, the more often and more thoroughly we need to be

The MRS. Ministry

reminded.

One of the things that I feel the need to be reminded of very often is the fact that God has put me in the ministry. "You mean you forget that your husband is a preacher?" No, that is not what I have trouble remembering. The thing that slips my mind most often is that God put me on this earth to serve Him, and that my whole purpose for living is to be what He wants me to be.

Now I don't exactly forget that this fact is true, but I *often* forget to let it occupy my mind and guide my thoughts, my words and my actions. Everything that I am, every role that I fill, every person in my life, every job that I have to do is part of the ministry that God has called me to fulfill.

That sounds good when you say it, doesn't it? The problem is that it doesn't always look that good when I try to live it. I can get 'amnesia' very quickly when facing my least favorite job or person and I really don't want to remember that I have an obligation to the Lord to 'minister' and to do what I'm doing 'as unto the Lord'.

I heard a preacher say, "There is no division between secular and sacred. For the child of God, all ground is holy ground." This is the area where it seems to hit me the hardest. Every place I go, every person in my life, every job I tackle, I should do ALL to glorify God. It's hard to yell at your children for the glory of God, isn't it? I've

Making The Most Of Your Ministry

found out that it's not any easier to avoid the people who make me miserable, so I won't feel obligated to treat them in a Christ-like manner. The Holy Spirit just seems to follow me around, and say, "Is that what Jesus would do?" Being reminded that my life IS a ministry sure changes the way things look to me.

Have you stopped to realize that you have a ministry, that your life IS a ministry? You say, "Not me, I don't preach, I don't teach, I don't sing, all I do is wash dishes and change diapers and scrub floors." There's a hint about the nature of your ministry. Or maybe you're saying, "I know I'm in the ministry on Sunday. That's when I teach a class, run a bus route, keep the nursery, and sing in the choir. I don't have any trouble with my ministry, it's my life that's giving me trouble!"

Let me give you a little reminder that you're in the ministry 24 hours a day, seven days a week. If you're saved, you're in the "Master Ministry". If you have a husband, you're in the "Marriage Ministry". If you have children, you're in the "Motherhood Ministry". If you belong to a local, New Testament church, you have a "Membership Ministry". If you live in a neighborhood, that's in a city, that's in a state, that's in a country, that's in a world full of people dying without the Gospel, you have a "Multitude Ministry."

I could go on, but are you beginning to get the picture? Every area of your daily life, every person that God has brought into your life, every job or responsibility that you face, presents you with your mission field, your opportunities to serve the Lord. Now THAT could seriously change the way we live, couldn't it?

Every woman reading this has a ministry just as important, just as demanding, just as life-changing as Dr. Hyles, Dr. Roberson, Dr. Malone, or any other important-sounding man you know of. Now I realize that the call to preach and to pastor is a very high calling that we should respect and follow, and I'm not trying to diminish that in the least. What I am trying to do is help you to realize that your ministry is just as important, and whether or not you fulfill it for the glory of God is going to seriously affect the lives of the people you love most.

Realize the importance of the ministry that God has given to YOU. It is just as wrong for us to be lax, careless, unconcerned, half-hearted, and unprepared about carrying out our ministry as it would be for any preacher you can name. You ought to put the same thought, ingenuity, prayer, creativity, concern, time and investment of yourself in your ministry as the pastor of the world's largest church or the highest paid executive in the world's largest corporation. This is life-changing! This is urgent! This is eternal! The most important ministry in the whole world

Making The Most Of Your Ministry
is YOURS!

Realizing that we are in the ministry can help us to be more dedicated in doing what we do. It can also help us to remain faithful and not quit on God.

I saw a family just this week of a lady who became involved with another man at her job and left her husband and children. Now her husband is trying to be both father and mother, help the kids to get through the emotional turmoil they're facing and trying to hold himself together since he's emotionally shipwrecked, too. Her children are heartbroken, just pictures of sadness and rejection.

This is a wife and mother who has 'quit the ministry'. I mean she quit serving God in the jobs that He gave her to do. For years she's been searching for something 'fulfilling and rewarding' to spend her life doing, while the most important job in the world went unheeded right under her nose and was neglected.

Why can't she see the value of being a wife and mother? If she could back up a few years and realize what I'm reminding us of right now, and let it become a reality in her life instead of just a spiritual-sounding motto, I guarantee you that her story would have a much happier ending.

Does this sound like a remote and uncommon story to you? I wish it were. I'm hearing it like a broken record so often that it

The M.R.S. Ministry

scares me to death. The devil is chipping away at the very foundations of the home and family so relentlessly that the American family will soon sound like an antique heirloom.

You and I need to see the importance of our own ministries a long way before we get to the point where we feel like quitting on God, and quitting on the people we love. With the Lord's help, I'd like to cover a few of these areas in the 'reminder mode', and refresh our memories about these avenues of serving Him.

The Priority

Notice that word -- "priority". The fact that it is singular and not plural means there can only be one priority. I heard Brother Lonnie Mattingly say this in a sermon, and it has helped me to refocus many times. He said, "The very word PRIORITY means 'the most important thing, the one at the top of the list, in first place'.

"Just like a superlative, best, biggest, most, highest, it signifies the fact that there can only be one. The sermons you hear about 'Organizing Your 10,000 Priorities" may sound good, but you can't have all of them in first place. Only one 'most important' thing can take first place above everything else in our lives, and the Lord has already chosen it for us."

So what is that one priority at the top of the

list? *"But seek ye first the kingdom of God, and his righteousness; and all these things shall be added unto you."* (Matthew 6:33) Notice also that this priority does not *exclude* every area of our lives, but rather it *encompasses* every area of our lives. It simply means that I put the Lord and His will first in every situation, in every task, and in every problem.

The Lord reworded this same priority for us in Matthew chapter 22. *"Then one of them, which was a lawyer, asked him a question, tempting him, and saying, Master, which is the great commandment in the law? Jesus said unto him, Thou shalt love the Lord thy God with all thy heart, and with all thy soul, and with all thy mind. This is the first and great commandment. And the second is like unto it, Thou shalt love thy neighbor as thyself. On these two commandments hang all the law and the prophets."* (Matthew 22:36-40) Someone asked him a question, hoping that Jesus would pick one responsibility or command out of all the others. Rather, Jesus gave him a command which included all the others, and focused them toward one goal. The priority is that God comes first in my life.

That doesn't mean we should live at the church and neglect our families. It doesn't mean that we are to go soulwinning 24 hours a day, and never complete our tasks as a wife and mother. It means that every area of our lives ought to

The MRS. Ministry

revolve around and be balanced on this central fulcrum --- love for the Lord Jesus Christ. Loving Him, and doing what He wants me to do in every area is first and foremost in my life. You can't be a good wife or mother without first being a good Christian. If Christ is not first in your life, your whole life is out of focus and off track. This one area pulls all other areas on center.

My husband says, "There are enough hours in every day to do everything that God wants me to do." There have been times when I felt like that couldn't possibly be true, and yet I know that God is the one who gave me each of these roles, each of these people, each of these jobs to do. He wants me to do everything that I do because I love Him. He wants me to do everything that I do empowered by Him. He wants me to do everything that I do as if I were standing in His presence doing it for Him, because I am!

The Lord knows that I can't go soulwinning and teach my children their schoolwork at the same time, and He is the One who gave me both of those responsibilities. If I will let Him, He'll show me how to balance my time and effort in both those areas, so that I'm pleasing Him in everything. I don't have to win any awards, I don't have to impress anyone, I just have to know in my heart that I'm doing my best, and letting Him handle the consequences.

Have you ever said, "What a relief!" Well,

that is the biggest relief I have ever felt, knowing that it all falls under the same category, and I don't have to feel like excelling in one area makes me a failure in every other area. Just do it all for Him, give it all to Him, and let the Lord balance the scales for you.

God's will for us is to become more like Jesus. *"For whom he did foreknow, he also did predestinate to be conformed to the image of his Son, that he might be the firstborn among many brethren."* (Romans 8:29) Our job is just to be Christlike, and *"do always those things that please the Father"*. Do you want to please the Lord in your life? Are you not sure how to serve God in the family and in the church where God put you? Just seek to do what Jesus would do with your responsibilities and the set of needs and circumstances that He has allowed you to face.

I think we do ourselves, our families, and our churches a great injustice when we do not see our ministry to them as a ministry. We miss big opportunities just because we're not looking for them. Let's take that text verse literally for ourselves, and examine our lives in light of its truth. *"...Take heed to the ministry which thou hast received in the Lord, that thou fulfil it."* (Colossians 4:17)

Our Ministry to Our Maker

Chapter Two

"...Take heed to the ministry which thou hast received in the Lord, that thou fulfil it."
(Colossians 4:17)

If you flip the channels on the TV and stop for a few moments on some talk show, you'll often see a row of people seated on the stage. Maybe it's a group of 'punk rockers' or 'skin heads' who are talking back against society's unwillingness to sanction their insane appearance and behavior. Maybe it's a group of rebellious teenagers with their equally rebellious parents fighting over rock music, premarital sex, insane dress, makeup and hair styles. You might see anything on one of those shows that will shock you out of your shoes.

But an underlying theme in so many of these conversations goes something like this. "I'm just trying to be myself and express who I am. I want to be different, and it's not fair that these other people won't accept me the way I am." But if you take another look, you'll notice that the people in these groups don't look different ... they look amazingly alike.

If you walk through a mall in almost any city, you'll start to notice that the same crazy looking hair styles and immoral, unbelievably ugly dress styles keep passing you by ... installed on different people. After you watch people for a while in an airport or some other public traffic jam, you might begin to think that many of those beings dropped off the end of the same assembly line. They look amazingly alike, yet they all claim, "I'm just trying to be different!"

I think God must have planted deep inside us a need to be individual, to have a special place and significance just for ourselves. We want to hold a specific place of worth in life that only we can fill. There is certainly nothing wrong with that innate longing, especially when you stop to realize that God is the author of individuality.

Only God would go to the pains of making every one of the billions and billions of snowflakes that fall completely distinct and different from every other one. Only God would plan for every fingerprint on every finger on every hand on every person to be clearly distinguishable from all others. Individuality is something only God can engineer, but as always, the devil has his counterfeit, and he goes to great pains to sell us the lie.

While the world swallows the devil's hook and goes to the farthest extremes to 'be different' or 'break out of the mold' they end up looking and acting like so many millions of paper dolls cut from the same pattern.

But when you and I as Christian ladies take the same Bible, the same commands from God, the same role and pattern we find for womanhood, the home, marriage and motherhood in the Bible, we miraculously become as unique and different as an individual snowflake. The more we mature and grow and become what God wants us to be, the more our uniqueness and differences stand out and mark us as 'one-of-a-kind'.

Nobody else can be what God wants you to be, or do what God wants you to do. You do have a vital and valuable place in the plan of God, and that longing in your heart can't be met in any other place if you'd search for it for a hundred years. For you to refuse or make excuse or disqualify yourself from fulfilling your ministry means that something specific God wants done will go undone, and needs in people's lives will go unmet.

"But I can't be Mrs. Hyles or Mrs. Evans" or whoever else you may name. You're right, and you shouldn't be. God wants to use YOU. If you could be that person that you admire, there would be a very important job left undone, and place left unfilled. YOURS! That doesn't mean we can't learn from the example and teaching and leadership of others --- we're supposed to. But we should not play-act at being a carbon copy of someone else, no matter how much we may admire them. We should learn from them and then incorporate those lessons and principles into our own lives and ministries. I need to serve God doing the thing I can do best, just being me.

Our good friend, Brother Jim Brown, has often made the statement, "That may be okay for so-and-so, but I'm glad God doesn't expect me to be him. I just like being me." God didn't make a mistake when He made you to be you instead of someone else. It's time we stop making excuses and begin to exult and rejoice in just being who God made us to be and doing what God made us to do.

Our Ministry To Our Maker

I guess that just naturally leads our train of thought into the first ministry that I want to remind us of --- the ministry that we have to the Lord Himself. "What do you mean --- my ministry to the Lord?" I mean that God has given us the opportunity to minister to Him, to meet needs that He has, to commune with His heart and share His thoughts and desires and yearnings.

"What do you mean, saying I'm supposed to meet God's needs? God is perfect, and complete. He doesn't have needs, and if He did, He could just speak and create whatever He needed." You're right! And that's exactly what He did! *"And God said, Let us make man in our image, after our likeness:... So God created man in his own image, in the image of God created he him; male and female created he them... And the* L<small>ORD</small> *God formed man of the dust of the ground, and breathed into his nostrils the breath of life; and man became a living soul."* (Genesis 1:26-27; 2:7)

In Revelation 4:11, we find out more about the purpose for which God created us: *"Thou art worthy, O Lord, to receive glory and honour and power: for thou hast created all things, and for thy pleasure they are and were created."* We were made for God to enjoy, and to ascribe glory, honor and power to Him. Consider this thought along with it. First Timothy 6:17 describes the Lord as *"...God...who giveth us richly all things to enjoy;"* God made all things for me to enjoy, but He made me for Him to enjoy.

The supernatural, all-powerful, all-knowing, eternal God DID have a need, and He DID speak that answer into existence. We are that answer. How can we minister to our Maker? Now, in this area I'm definitely a pre-schooler peering into a post-graduate classroom, but I have a few ideas of how we can get started carrying out this part of our ministry.

Much of our service as ladies is ministering

Ministry To Our Maker

to other people for God. But the ways in which we can minister to God and be a blessing to His heart are wrapped up in our personal devotional life, the time that we spend alone with God in prayer and communion, worship and adoration, when we can spend a little while being consumed with just Who God is, and how wonderful and beyond understanding and explanation He is, the times that we reflect on the fathomless depths of God's love for us, and let it turn our hearts to love Him more than ever.

I've heard my husband say something like this, "Soulwinning is important, and we're not in any danger of taking it too seriously. But that's not our primary purpose in life. You see, God didn't create a man and woman and place them in the Garden to go soulwinning. There was no need for soulwinning, because there was no sin. But rather, God made mankind in His image and communed with them daily to meet His need to love and to be loved. He created man to serve Him, to walk with Him, to love and adore Him.

"Once sin separated mankind from His Creator, then there arose a need for us to have a 'ministry of reconciliation', of making peace between God and man and restoring their original intended relationship so that human beings could once again fulfill the purpose for which they were created. We don't just go soulwinning to keep people from going to hell, although that's one very important reason. We also go soulwinning so that people can fulfill their purpose for life, to love God, to walk with Him and serve Him."

God needs our love and devotion. He deserves it. He should be able to expect it. But how often are we just 'too busy'. Someone rightly said, "If you're too busy to spend time with God, then you're TOO busy." Love God. Worship God. Talk to God. Depend on Him. Adore Him. Meditate on Him. Praise Him. Give to Him.

"But I really am very busy." So am I, and I fail so often in this respect that I'd be ashamed to say. But I realize that when I get my heart in touch with the heart of God, my mind in tune with the mind of Christ, then I tap unlimited resources on a totally different plane that I have no access to otherwise. What I gain through that supernatural communion gives me the strength and love and wisdom and power I desperately need to fulfill all of the other ministries that I have.

Martha's mistake is one that I seem to make over and over again. The tragic mistake of work without worship, service without devotional life. *"Now it came to pass, as they went, that he entered into a certain village: and a certain woman named Martha received him into her house. And she had a sister called Mary, which also sat at Jesus' feet, and heard his word. But Martha was cumbered about much serving, and came to him, and said, Lord, dost thou not care*

Ministry To Our Maker

that my sister hath left me to serve alone? bid her therefore that she help me. And Jesus answered and said unto her, Martha, Martha, thou art careful and troubled about many things: But one thing is needful: and Mary hath chosen that good part, which shall not be taken away from her." (Luke 10:38-42)

I also catch myself doing the Lord's work without sitting at the Lord's feet, and just like Martha, I get the grumbles. When we first spend time looking at the wonderful grace of God, and adoring our blessed Saviour, then no task seems too great, no matter who else helps or doesn't help. I just want to demonstrate my uncontainable love for Him. But when my eyes haven't been on Him, then they tend to get riveted on other people, who disappoint me and fail to live up to my expectations. God certainly expects us to do His work, but work without worship is a costly mistake, and often a fatal one.

What are we doing to fulfill our ministry to our Maker? Is it time to re-evaluate our personal devotion and worship of the Lord that no one sees but Him? This is the private part of ourselves that no one else will reward us or commend us for, yet it is the very core of true Christianity. My heart has smitten me again and again in considering the subject, but this is the first and foremost segment of my life's ministry.

"Thou shalt love the Lord thy God with all thy heart, and with all thy soul, and with all thy

The MRS. Ministry

mind. This is the first and great commandment."

Why God Made A Man

*How disappointed God must be
Each day that he looks down to see
Us busy racing here and there,
Amidst the hurried thoroughfare.
In His work we're all consumed,
Yet God Himself can find no room
In our stressful come and go;
And our neglect must hurt Him so.*

*No time for the Bible? No time to pray?
No time to spend with the Lord today?
How short we have fallen, we've missed the goal
Of why God made man a living soul.
For when He chose to make mankind,
It was not because He couldn't find
Someone to rush and fret and strive
To help Him keep His work alive.*

*But rather the need of God's great heart
Was for someone to share a part
Of all His love; for God's one lack
Was the need for someone to love Him back.
And so God made man without sin
To walk and talk each day with Him
To love, adore and serve the Lord,
To learn and live His precious Word.*

Ministry To Our Maker
Yet how quickly we can find,
Other loves to take our time
While we have no time or attention for
The One who loved us so much more.
Love created and love redeemed,
Love so infinite that it seems
God's heart must break over our great sin
When we've time for His work, but no time for Him.
(---Cathy Corle)

Our Ministry In Marriage

Chapter Three

"...Take heed to the ministry which thou hast received in the Lord, that thou fulfil it."
(*Colossians 4:17*)

We've been looking at the different areas in the life of a Christian lady, and considering all the different aspects of her 'ministry'. God gives a pastor to a church and a church to a pastor, and he is responsible to oversee many different parts of the ministry. The soulwinning outreach, bus ministry, Sunday School, youth department, Christian School or Bible Institute (if that church has one,) and maybe more areas that you can think of --- these are not all separate ministries, but different aspects of the same ministry, with the same purpose.

The church's purpose is to win souls, baptize converts, and disciple believers to grow in grace and the knowledge of our Lord Jesus Christ. That is the Great Commission. All these ministries are just different avenues to carry out this purpose.

Ministry In Marriage

In the same way, our lives as Christian ladies branch out into several different 'ministries', but it really has just one central purpose: to love the Lord with all our heart and to serve Him faithfully and put Him in first place in everything. My whole life is a ministry to serve the Lord in the place where He has put me, with the people that He has given to me, and in the areas where the Lord has given me opportunity and ability.

After the Lord Himself, the most important person that God has given to me is that man I looked at when I said, "I do." There is no one else in the whole world that I have more obligation to minister and meet needs for than my husband. He is the reason why God put me here.

"And the LORD God said, It is not good that the man should be alone; I will make him an help meet for him... And the LORD God caused a deep sleep to fall upon Adam, and he slept: and he took one of his ribs, and closed up the flesh instead thereof; And the rib, which the LORD God had taken from man, made he a woman, and brought her unto the man. And Adam said, This is now bone of my bones, and flesh of my flesh: she shall be called Woman, because she was taken out of Man. Therefore shall a man leave his father and his mother, and shall cleave unto his wife: and they shall be one flesh." (Genesis 2:18,21-24) It is unscriptural and unhealthy for husbands and wives to go their own way and do

their own thing and live separate lives. God made us 'one flesh', and we're to live one life together and serve the Lord together as one.

I can hear someone thinking it right now. "Well, that may have been alright for Eve, but I have my own life to live. My husband is a big boy; he can take care of himself." No, that won't work. God told all wives, you and me included, to line up with the Bible. ***"Wives, submit yourselves unto your own husbands, as unto the Lord. For the husband is the head of the wife, even as Christ is the head of the church: and he is the saviour of the body. Therefore as the church is subject unto Christ, so let the wives be to their own husbands in every thing... Nevertheless let every one of you in particular so love his wife even as himself; and the wife see that she reverence her husband."*** *(Ephesians 5:22-24,33)*

Notice that it's not commanded of my husband to earn my respect and followship, although he should. The primary responsibility is put upon me to see that I submit to my husband's leadership and to see that I regard him with respect. "But he's not loving me like he's supposed to, so I don't have to submit to him either." Sorry, but it doesn't work that way.

You're not responsible to your husband for your submission. You're responsible to God, and you'll have to answer to Him. If my husband is not doing what he ought to do in our marriage, I am still obligated to obey the Lord, and that means to submit and respect my husband's leadership.

Now I have found this to be true: if I do what I'm supposed to do with the best attitude I can muster, God will honor that and start working on my husband about his side of the relationship. When I'm trying my best to do right and obey God in my marriage just because it's right, then I have a right to pray for God to do something in my husband's heart and expect a definite answer. I can't tell you how many times I've done just that, and how many sweet and wonderful answers the Lord has sent my way.

Please let me encourage you if you feel like you're in a tough spot in your marriage. Just decide to do right. You get your heart right, submit to your husband's leadership with respect and a right attitude, and do your best to love him and meet his needs. If you'll do that, you have a power greater than dynamite in your hands to do what you were already trying to do in the wrong way -- turn him into the kind of husband you've always wanted. You can't do it, but the Lord most definitely can. So you obey the Lord and talk with Him about it, and you'll be amazed at the results.

But what is submission? Does it mean that I'm supposed to demean myself and act like a doormat or a slave? No, not at all. It means that in this important enterprise called the family, my husband is the president, and I'm the vice president. We both have valuable input. We both have important duties and responsibilities. But when our opinions differ, he has the final decision.

When things are right between us, then we love one another and treat one another with kindness and courtesy, and you will rarely be able to tell when our opinions differ. Besides that, our hearts are both wrapped up in the same purpose and goal, to serve and please the Lord in the ministry He has given us together, and that keeps us thinking and moving in the same direction ninety-nine percent of the time with no major disagreements.

But then there are other times... You know what I mean! When the road gets rocky, then my part is submission and followship. I need to let my husband know what I think or feel about the situation, let him know that I'm praying the Lord will help him make the right decisions, and then be quiet and cooperative.

Husbands and wives occupy positions that are equal in importance, but different in responsibility. My husband has often illustrated followship by pointing out our truck and trailer. They are both important to us, and in some ways the trailer is probably more important. But that doesn't change the fact that when they're moving down the road, the truck is to lead and the trailer is to follow. If the trailer ever gets in the lead, it's going to destroy itself, and anything in its path.

Ministry In Marriage

That goes for us followers, too. Whether you're talking about pastor and church member, parent and child, or husband and wife, the follower in any relationship can only fulfill his important purpose if he stays in that rightful position. Even a good trailer following a poor truck is better off to stay in the position where it's supposed to be!

When you read the book of Ezekiel, you'll find that in eternity past, Satan was given great opportunity and important position. He was 'the anointed cherub that covereth' in the very Garden of God. He was created with great musical ability, and I've heard his position referred to as the great choir-master in Heaven.

But Lucifer refused to submit, and to stay in the place where God had put him. His heart was lifted up in pride, and he exalted himself against the very God of Heaven. His rebellion made a devil out of him. It prefaced all the sin and misery and destruction that this world has ever known. His sin was serious. Could it be just as serious for us to be dissatisfied with our position and thrust ourselves into authority not meant for us?

The last thing I want to mention is a rather encouraging thought, as far as I'm concerned. Submission is quite unnatural to our sinful human nature. It only becomes possible with Spirit-fullness and Christlikeness. In Ephesians 5:18 we read the command, *"...Be filled with the Spirit."* It is *after* this command that we receive the command that says, *"Wives, submit yourselves unto your own husbands, as unto the Lord."* (*verse 22*)

You may be discouraged and think, "Why is it so easy for other wives, and so hard for me? Is it just because of my husband that it's so hard to submit to him? Or is it just because of everything that's wrong with me that I'm having such a hard time with it?"

No, it's because we're all sinners, and it comes much easier to our sinful nature to rebel and exert authority than to submit. The devil encourages our sinful flesh to exalt itself, and only the sweet and blessed influence of the Holy Spirit in my life makes it possible to do what goes against my sinful nature and submit. Only the Holy Spirit in my life produces a 'meek and quiet spirit', and makes it not only possible but enjoyable to occupy the place that God has given me in my marriage.

Remember, too, that these verses we've been reading precede those in Ephesians six that describe the spiritual warfare that goes on in our daily lives, that many of us are completely oblivious to. I am convinced that many of our marriage difficulties are not homemade, but part of Satan's very subtle and very successful plot to destroy our marriages and to turn us against one another. If we could see now, as I'm sure we will at the Judgement Seat of Christ, just how often it was the devil who was to blame rather than our husbands, I think it would shock us. It also would remind us to be more prayerful and more watchful over our marriage and over our own spirit and attitude.

Make up your mind to do right in your marriage. As a wife, I'm responsible to God to submit to my husband's leadership. When I do so, I'm obeying God, no matter what my husband does. When I refuse, I'm in direct disobedience to the God of Heaven, no matter what my husband does. His wrong never justifies my wrong.

But if I'll do right, no matter how hard it sometimes seems, God will honor it and answer my heart's prayer and deepest need in giving me the kind of husband he wanted me to have when He said, **"Husbands, love your wives, even as Christ also loved the church, and gave himself for it;"** (Ephesians 5:25)

My first and most important ministry after my relationship to the Lord is my ministry to my husband, to be what he needs and to serve the Lord together with him. To even get started in the right direction to fulfill this ministry, I need to be in submission to my husband's leadership. Instead of 'putting him in his place', like we're often tempted to do, I need to put myself in my place, following my husband as he follows God.

I hope these thoughts have been an

The MRS. Ministry

encouragement and help to you like they have been for me. Please follow along as we come back and examine more about your ministry in marriage to the most important man in the world --- your husband.

Your Ministry in Marriage - Continued

Chapter Four

"...Take heed to the ministry which thou hast received in the Lord, that thou fulfil it."
(Colossians 4:17)

In the ways that your husband is unique and individual, your ministry to him as 'helpmeet' or completer is unique. He is one of a kind. There is no other man in the world who is just like him. He has a unique background and upbringing, and the Lord has worked in his life differently than any other man you know.

His personality is unique. He has different strengths and weaknesses in his life. God's purpose for him and leading is different than from other men that God is using in other ways. Just as your husband is unique, his needs for a 'completer' or helpmeet might differ from other husbands.

So your ministry to him and the ways in which you help can not be exactly the same as every other wife you know. Isn't that a relief?

"But I can't play the piano like Mrs. So and So. I don't know how to type. I'm not a very good ladies' group leader, like my friend is." God gave you to your husband because he's special, and because you're special.

God has made (and is making) you exactly suited to him. You're not supposed to be like Mrs. So and So. Your husband probably doesn't need all the exact same things in the exact same way that her husband needs and wants. So forget all your previous prejudices about what 'a good preacher's wife does', or what any wife does, and concentrate on what the Bible says and what your husband needs.

"That they may teach the young women to be sober, to love their husbands, to love their children, To be discreet, chaste, keepers at home, good, obedient to their own husbands, that the word of God be not blasphemed." (Titus 2:4-5) While there are many passages in the Bible that deal with a wife's ministry, I personally think these verses give us a good representation of what the Bible teaches ladies about their marriage responsibilities.

Let's examine what this passage has to say about what you and I ought to be. Here is the first: Be sober, or take your job seriously. Be the best you can for your husband.

LOVE YOUR HUSBAND, that's the biggest part of the job, and show him constantly that you

Ministry In Marriage

love him. Love him enough to try to be what he needs in every area of life.

Love your children. God put the two of us together, as president and vice-president of this important institution called the Corle Home. One of the most important jobs of our home is to raise our children in the nurture and admonition of the Lord, and train them to love and serve the Lord with all their heart.

I have a special place as 'mom', to be the emotional support, the kisser of boo-boos, the watchful eye for everybody's welfare, spiritually and emotionally as well as physically. I get to administer hugs and kisses, as well as the occasional spanking or 'good talking to'. These are some of the ways that I can carry out my responsibility to love my children.

Be discreet and chaste. While these words have their own definitions and connotations, I am going to put them together. Be pure and clean in your thoughts as well as your actions in the presence of all other men. Let it be known loud and clear that you belong only to your husband, and you're glad that you do.

Don't allow yourself to become close friends with men, whether married or single. Avoid dangerous situations being alone with another man, and situations that could look questionable to others, even if you know they are not.

The MRS. Ministry

Your love on every plane, physically, emotionally, and spiritually, is a special gift that God has allowed you to GIVE to your husband and to GUARD for your husband. While you should be friendly and Christian in your relationship to all others, you should also be proper and clearly defined as 'unavailable'. Every thing about you ought to point out, "I belong to him."

God also commanded us to be 'keepers at home'. That means that the primary responsibility for the duties in the home belongs to the wife. Remember that our home is an institution established by God.

One of the needs in our home is financial support. Some married couples run a farm or a family business to meet this need. Others 'sell their time' by being employed by another person's business in order to secure the finances needed in their home.

I think the Bible is clear that the responsibility of financial provision belongs primarily to the husband. *"But if any provide not for his own, and specially for those of his own house, he hath denied the faith, and is worse than an infidel."* (I Timothy 5:8)

If a wife does make money toward the family finances, on her own or at a conventional job site, she is simply 'helping' her husband to fulfill his responsibility. This should be done only if both partners agree that it is best, and in an environment that is safe for the wife and poses no problem in her being able to carry out her responsibilities in the marriage.

By the same token, 'home keeping', or the responsibilities that center in the home, are given primarily to the wife. They come to mind very quickly. Cooking, cleaning, laundry, childcare, etc.

It's not wrong for a husband to help with the dishes or cleaning, especially in times of exceptional busyness and stress or maybe illness. Maybe he just wants to prove that he loves her, and he does a special job just to be a blessing and to help lift the load. But being the keeper of the home is assigned to the wife first of all, and in normal, everyday circumstances, she needs to accept that as her responsibility.

Be good. Sounds kind of oversimplified, doesn't it? But that's what God said. Good as opposed to bad, doing right instead of doing wrong. Be good not only in what you do, but in what you are. Become a genuine, sincere, godly, Christian in the kind of person that you are, the kind of personality that you exhibit in the way that you live your life as a wife as well as a believer.

God is good, and we are to become as much like Him as we can be, and to develop in our own lives the qualities of goodness that we learn from Him and from His Word.

Obedient unto MY own husband? Surely God wasn't talking to you and me, was He? Yes, He certainly was! God also knew that our husbands would be as far from perfect as we are when He issued this command. One of my famous sayings has become, "It isn't always easy, but it is always right."

My husband has been commanded to love me, to protect me, to provide for me, and to lead me according to God's leading for him. My God-given responsibility is to love my husband, to follow his leadership, and to support him and encourage him and assist him in everything God calls him to do.

There's no conditional trapdoor. "Well, if he's doing his part, then I'll do mine." I must do what God commanded for me to do, do it 'as unto the Lord', and pray about the Lord dealing with my husband in the areas where I may think he falls short. God can handle it. He's proved that to me time and time again.

"...that the word of God be not blasphemed." That still sounds as scary to me today as it did the first time I read it! To think that my actions or failures as a wife, mother and homemaker could actually have such an impact as to blaspheme God's Word!

It sounds serious, and it is. But every time I see another broken home and the broken promises, broken hearts and broken lives that go with it, I understand why God said that all over again. Marriage is serious business, it's God's business, and we need to give ourselves wholeheartedly to making it work, and to seeing God's blessing on our lives and relationships.

Now, while that's not an exhaustive study of God's commands to wives in the marriage relationship, I hope that we've touched on the most important points. Once I am doing my best to be what GOD COMMANDS from a wife, then I need to turn my eyes in the direction of what MY HUSBAND NEEDS in HIS wife.

When you married your husband you probably experienced the desire to be able to cook his favorite things. So what did you do, get a list from 10,000 different wives of their husbands' favorite recipes, and hold yourself to a tight schedule of mastering them all in your first week of marriage? No, you were smarter than that. Here's what you probably did.

"Honey, what would you like me to make for supper?" (Batting eyelashes.) "Oh, it doesn't matter, anything you make will be good." (Big smile.) "But dear, what is your FAVORITE meal? I want to cook the thing that you like best," you pleaded with more batting of the eyelashes. "Well, I like lots of different things, but..." "What is it?!? Hurry and tell me! I want to know!" "Well, I don't know if it's my very favorite, but one

The MRS. Ministry

thing I've always liked is..." and he named some dish that he liked. "Well, that's what we're having for dinner tonight!" you said. As soon as he walked out the door, you called your mother and said, "Help mom! I have to know how to fix..." or better yet, you called his mom, and asked how she fixed it that he liked it so well.

That sounds a lot easier than the 10,000 recipes in a week, doesn't it? And if you tried the 10,000 recipe routine your husband would wonder by the end of the week if you're trying to a) kill him quickly with overeating so you can collect his insurance policy or b) win some homemaker of the year award to impress all your friends or c) have a nervous breakdown in record time so you can tell him that cooking is too much pressure for you.

In 99 out of 100 brains in the male species, I guarantee that they would never interpret all that to say, "I love you. I want to be what you need. I want to make you happy and do things the way you like them."

But should you take the batting-of-the-eyelashes-and-big-smile route, even a man could get the message loud and clear, and I think he'd understand your intentions even if supper gets burned to a crisp and you end up at Kentucky Fried Chicken!

You see, it really isn't all that hard. He married you because he decided that he loved you

Ministry In Marriage

and couldn't live without you. He doesn't want you to be like Mrs. So-and-so. He wants you to keep being like the girl he fell in love with. Since you've already won first place and only place in that contest, you can begin, one thing at a time, to find out what he needs and what he desires, then try to incorporate those things into your marriage relationship.

First meet his needs as a man, then as a preacher, or businessman, or whatever your husband is. Although I'm sure I've always had that in order in my brain, I'm also sure that it's gotten out of order many times in my actions. I know there have been times that I have been so consumed in being a part of my husband's ministry that I came home completely exhausted or upset or stressed out, or maybe even too excited or preoccupied to be the kind of wife he needed and wanted to have when he got home.

I need to remind myself that I'm a wife first, and a preacher's wife second. His needs for companionship, support and understanding, for a 'homey', restful atmosphere, for an affectionate and loving wife should come first, before the demands of his ministry.

You can become the kind of wife that your husband needs. Moreover, you're the only one in the world who can! You have an important ministry and a challenging opportunity in this wonderful thing called marriage. That man that you married needs someone very much. It's not

The MRS. Ministry

Superwife or Wonder Woman. It's not a clone of Mrs. So and So, who keeps coming to your mind and discouraging you because you could never be just like her. He needs the loving ministry of someone very special that God made just for him --- YOU.

Our Ministry In Marriage - Continued

Chapter Five

"...Take heed to the ministry which thou hast received in the Lord, that thou fulfil it."
(Colossians 4:17)

Marriage is an unending assignment, a life-long adventure, and a continually growing, living, becoming relationship. Because it is God-designed and God-ordained, marriage is inherently good and godly and spiritual in its nature. But because it is just that, it is under the most vehement attack by the forces of hell, maybe even more than our churches.

Just because the devil often disguises his devious deeds so that we lay the blame on each other doesn't make his attack any less evil. In fact, that's his most successful plot. Instead of husband and wife standing together against his obvious onslaught, he deceitfully gets us to to turn our anger against one another, and he wins.

I guess that's why I feel such a burden to encourage and challenge ladies in this area. It's certainly not because I feel qualified to tell everyone else how it ought to be! But while I motivate myself and try to discover just what God wants me to do in my marriage, let me share a few of the things that I'm learning with you.

Not only is the idea of being married part of God's plan, but God has a specific plan about every area of that relationship. The closer I can get to that ideal, the more sweet and secure and fulfilling that relationship will become in my life.

The farther I wander from God's principles in marriage, though, the more dangerous and destructive my actions will be upon my marriage. While my marriage is made up of two people who both have plenty of faults, I don't want to lose sight of what God means for it to be, and what God is well able to make it become.

Just the other day I was talking with a friend, and I encouraged her to read a book that I thought could encourage her in a particular area. Her response was, "I quit reading those books because I can do all that stuff, and I'd be glad to, but he doesn't want to and won't let me." I said, "Well, I know it's a long way from where you are to there, but I think you might find something in it that would unlock a door, or help you to understand his needs or even his hurts, and then you could come back to it again later to get the rest."

Rather than letting this ideal relationship

Ministry In Marriage

be a measuring stick that causes me to despair and quit trying, I need to keep it in sight as a goal that I'm aiming for.

While I'm continually seeing God's ideal relationship, I should also be looking at my marriage realistically, seeing where we are today, and figuring out what I should work on next to make it more like it ought to be. While I'm looking at where we are in comparison with where we ought to be, my goal should be to constantly see that gap closing, and those two pictures looking more and more alike.

And while we're on that subject, let me remind you of this, as well. It used to be very discouraging to me that while I was intent upon building a great marriage, my husband seemed too busy to do any more than just be glad that I wanted to. But I realized one day that God gave a man a work to do, and then gave him a wife to help him in that work. While marriage is important and vital to the husband, it is not his life's work, and so it can't consume the majority of his time and energy.

But being his wife IS my life's work, so no wonder I take it more seriously. Therefore, I shouldn't let myself become so disappointed when his energies are not poured into that endeavor to the same extent as mine. That helped me very much not to expect more than is fair, and consequently helped me to be pleased with every act of giving he makes in our relationship, instead of always feeling disillusioned because it's not more.

Some things are the same in every marriage, and we covered much of that previously in looking at God's commands for every wife. But some characteristics and needs differ with every marriage, and that has to do with the differences in every man, and how our personalities mesh together in this 'one-flesh' relationship. In those ways, our relationship may be quite unique.

It has been said that opposites attract, and my, oh my, is that ever true! I used to think that God designed it that way because He just loves to watch a good fight! But I realized one day that if we truly allow the Holy Spirit to fill and control us, God will take that chemistry of differences to blend our lives into one and allow his strengths to balance my weaknesses, and vice versa.

Just think, if two very talkative people ended up married to each other, who would ever listen? And if two quiet, withdrawn people are bound in holy matrimony, how will one ever find out from the other what day the garbage should go out? It's somewhat natural that a person is attracted to someone who is strong in the area where he is weak, and I think God must have decided that it is best, too.

Your husband has weaknesses, and if you

haven't discovered them yet, don't worry --- you will! You could complain about them to him and to the whole world. You could criticize and belittle him for his faults. Many of the ways that wives commonly respond to their husbands failures and faults are destructive to their relationship.

But you could pray about them, too, you know. You could look for ways that you could magnify his strengths and draw attention away from the sore spots. If you'll decide to really love him, it will show in how you respond to the things you like the least about him.

God has given me the special opportunity to accept my husband as he is, and then help him to become what he should be and could be. If your husband lacks confidence, then it's your job to build him up, admire him, encourage him, convince him that you believe in him and help him believe in himself.

If he is less aware of the needs and feelings of other people, and you have a knack at picking up on those things, then you can be his perceptive eyes and help him to see the things that he would otherwise miss.

If he is easily discouraged and defeated, then don't belittle him for it, but lift him up, help him to see from a different perspective, and provide some diversion as well as some inspiration.

The M.R.S. Ministry

You can learn to help compensate for his needs in many ways, and don't forget to let him shine in his strengths. If he's bold as a bulldog and just as determined, don't discourage him in that area. Pray that the Lord will teach him to direct that strength in the right avenues, and to temper and mold his personality to be more Christlike.

Don't be quiet about all the positives in your husband's life, while being loud and clear about the negatives. Be his cheerleader. Be on his side, rooting for him, and just cheer louder whenever he's down. Convince him that you believe in him, and help him to be able to believe in himself.

Whatever I do to help my husband find a right balance ought to be creative and edifying, never destructive. How does my husband view my attempts at 'completing' him? Am I really encouraging or just nagging? Don't forget that *"A continual dropping in a very rainy day and a contentious woman are alike"* (Proverbs 27:15) *"It is better to dwell in the corner of the housetop, than with a brawling woman and in a wide house."* (Proverbs 25:24)

Be positive, even in negative situations. Learn the art of creative communication. Anything that really needs to be said, can be said in a helping, healing, edifying way.

I enjoyed Cindy Schaap's book <u>A Wife's</u>

Ministry In Marriage

Purpose immensely, and I felt one of the most valuable things she had to say was the comparison between nagging or completing your husband. She said that completing equals prayer plus praise plus action. Instead of nagging my husband about the needs I see in his life, I ought to first pray about it, then praise him for every step I see him take in the right direction, and also take action in any way that I can assist him or make it easier for him to make that change.

Anything I do in this area of helping to 'balance out' my husband needs to be made up of 99% sugar and honey. If I'll keep my communication sweet, when I do have a legitimate complaint he'll be a lot more likely to listen to me.

The idea is to help bring him back on center, not to get my own way --- not for selfish reasons, but for the good of the whole family, his ministry, and also what's best for him. It's God's design that what is best is best for everyone, so if I'll get my eyes on what's best for my marriage and my family, I'll also be rewarded with what's best and happiest for me.

There are some things that every man needs, just because he's a man. So let me mention those needs briefly. I am going to mention five, and they are not necessarily in order of their importance. I have renamed and rearranged them somewhat to help me remember what they are by

The MRS. Ministry

starting with A, B, C, D & E.

A is for ADMIRATION. I don't care how confident and self-assured your husband is, he has an innate need for you to admire him. Admire him verbally. Admire him openly. Admire him in his work. Admire him in his character. Admire him in his good qualities. Admire him in his manly appearance.

He may not be able to admit to you, "I need that. I enjoy that." But he does. Man is made in the image of God, and God enjoys hearing us worship and adore Him, and tell Him how marvelous He is. Our husbands are no different. Though he may not be perfect, he needs to hear that he is perfect for you, and that you notice and appreciate all the good things about him.

While a wife needs to feel protected and cared for, a husband needs to feel that he is the strong protector. He needs to be needed as well as appreciated. Be sure he knows how much you admire him.

B is for a BEAUTIFUL WIFE. A man has a real desire and need for attractiveness and femininity in the woman he loves. It's more vital to a man than it is to a woman that he find his mate lovely, attractive, and appealing. Men are more visually oriented in their relationships, and how you look to him is an important factor.

Now, the words 'beautiful' and 'attractive' probably have somewhat different definitions between men and women. Women think of expensive clothing, flawless hairstyle, and impeccable makeup when they think of 'beautiful'.

But to most men, the word 'beautiful' might mean soft, feminine, or appealing. He probably doesn't care if the outfit came from Saks Fifth Avenue or Salvation Army as long as he finds it attractive. He didn't marry Miss America, and he doesn't expect you to look like her. But he probably does want you to try to look your best, and to be concerned about looking lovely just for him. He needs to find you beautiful.

C is for COMPANIONSHIP IN RECREATION . This was a real eye opener for me. While a woman craves deep, meaningful conversation and a bonding of souls in communication, a man enjoys that but has a greater need for companionship in doing rather than in talking. He needs someone to go to a ball game with, someone to go fishing or boating with, someone who enjoys doing together the kinds of things that he likes to do.

One of the biggest disappointments in a man's life is when he marries the girl who enjoyed doing everything with him that he always liked to do, and he was convinced they were so compatible. Then after the honeymoon he finds out that she really doesn't enjoy any of those things. She just did them to be with him. Now that she lives with him 24 hours a day, she no longer wants to go to the football game with him or to play volleyball, and he feels betrayed.

Your husband has a need for you enjoy with him some of the things that he enjoys. Be his companion and playmate and enjoy with him the things that he enjoys.

D is for DOMESTIC SUPPORT. This can mean several things. He needs to be able to go to his work and feel confident that she has things well under control at home. He needs to come home to a tranquil haven and a getaway from the pressures of his work, not to more pressure and more work. He needs to have a loving, healing atmosphere to come home to, not tension and arguing.

That's why it's special to him if you will meet him at the door with a kiss. That's why it means so much to him to come home and find that you've fixed his favorite meal, or prepared a snack tray just for his TV football game. It's not just a special 'extra' to him, but a real need.

Family involvement is more important to the wife, and she wants to feel that she and the children are important to him, that he wants to spend time with them and meet their needs. And he should do that. But he doesn't need that in the same way that his wife does. He needs her domestic support, her loving presence and provision for his needs at home.

Ministry In Marriage

E is for an EXCITING PHYSICAL RELATIONSHIP. A woman is far more likely to crave romance and emotional closeness. She needs to hear loving words and receive special gifts and sweet reminders of how much she is loved. Those things may be much more important to her than the actual physical relationship they share.

Her husband enjoys those things also, but his greater need is for the physical relationship to be sweet and special more than the emotional counterpart. Again, misunderstanding results when the wife says, "He never talks to me," and the husband says, "She never wants my attentions."

In each of these areas, there are two sides to the coin. Both partners need and want each side, but there is one side that will always win out with them, and it's usually opposite of what's most important to their mate. That is why we sometimes have such a hard time understanding one another, and sometimes feel hurt and betrayed when it is actually just a lack of understanding rather than a lack of caring.

I think we can solve a few of our marriage difficulties and avoid many more just by realizing that these needs differ between men and women. I can avoid thinking that my husband doesn't care about what is important to me, and instead take the time and effort to help him understand what

The MRS. Ministry

is important to me. I can see that his greatest need is different than mine, and concentrate on meeting his need rather than fretting over mine. Understanding our differences is the first big step in solving our differences.

Let me add just a few more thoughts. Let your husband make his mistakes. Since you didn't want to marry an 80 year old man who had already acquired all the wisdom life has to offer, you found yourself married to a young man who is much more attractive, even though he is much less wise. There are some things that he will insist on learning the hard way, so don't let it destroy your relationship with each other.

Let him make his mistakes, take his lumps, and go on with life. Some things he will be willing to learn about from another man, but he really doesn't want to hear it from his wife. Since he's the leader, he can't bear to feel like he's always following his wife's leadership.

Therefore, when you feel he's making a mistake and he doesn't seem to be listening to you, just pray about it, trust the Lord to make it all work out in the end, and make up your mind that you love him anyway.

Here's a vital thought to keep in view. Whatever it is that you're right about and he's wrong about is not nearly as important as your marriage, anyway. And besides, you may find out that he is the one who is right after all!

Ministry In Marriage

You'll find that the more you build him up and assure him that you have confidence in him through the years, the more he will be willing and even eager to hear your advice about life's decisions.

Be his wife, not his mother. You're his helpmeet, so your job is to help him do what God wants him to do with his life. Your job is not to do it for him. Don't handle his responsibility for him. Let him be the one responsible, and then make yourself available to 'help'.

If your husband never had the opportunity to grow up and handle responsibility and take the lead, don't continue to deprive him of it. Be willing to step back, follow his lead, and let him learn and grow. Don't mother over him and protect him and do everything for him. In time, you'll both come to resent that unnatural twist in your marriage. Let him be the man God meant him to be, and be patient and loving if you need to wait while he 'grows into' that role.

Become his best friend. Marriage is not just a physical union, and not just a uniting of two people's futures into one. It should be a oneness of heart, soul, mind and spirit as well. Most of us felt that before we were married. That was what caused us to feel that we couldn't live apart, that we needed to be together for always. There was a joining of our hearts.

But somewhere along the way, we may

have lost that aspect of being one flesh. We may have ceased to enjoy just being together and enjoying one another. I have a few little items that say, "Happiness is being married to your best friend." I want that to be a reality, and I think that's what God meant for marriage to be.

Have a vision of what God can do with your husband, and with the two of you together. As a teenager I read the story of D. L. Moody. Moody was probably the 'least likely to succeed' as far as outward appearances and qualifications. But he heard a preacher say, "It's yet to be seen what the Lord could do with a man wholly surrendered to him." The young Moody purposed in his heart, "By the grace of God, I will be that man." History tells us the miraculous results of that decision.

I thought, "The Bible teaches that man and wife are supposed to be 'one flesh' and serve God together as one. But I have never heard a challenge to see what God could do with one husband and wife who together yielded their lives totally to God." I was challenged to want to see that become a reality in my life and marriage. While I can't say that the Lord has used us in the same way that he used D. L. Moody, I can say that the Lord has used the most unlikely pair and done miraculous things in our life together.

Let me challenge you, too, to want to see what God can do with you as a 'one-flesh' partnership, giving your lives to serve Him. Be a

Ministry In Marriage

part of what God is doing in his life. Get involved and be excited about it.

You have a great opportunity to minister and meet needs and serve the Lord in your marriage. You have a ministry of encouragement, edification, followship, and being the wife that your husband has always dreamed of having. Though I've failed so often and so severely in my own life, I continually come back to that desire of my marriage being everything that God means for it to be, and I hope that you will, too.

*"It's yet to be seen what the Lord could do
With a man surrendered wholly, if his wife was, too;
With two who are truly one, a husband and a wife
Who give to God all their heart,
and give Him all their life.*

*The world has never truly seen what God meant us to be
But they might just get a glimpse
through the lives of you and me
Because it's yet to be seen what the Lord could do
With a man surrendered wholly — if his wife was, too."*

Our Ministry In Motherhood

Chapter Six

"...Take heed to the ministry which thou hast received in the Lord, that thou fulfil it."
(Colossians 4:17)

There are some very important people that live at your house. They sometimes make messes and break the family treasures. They track a lot of mud through the house, dirty a lot of laundry, and create more housework in a day than you can accomplish in a week. If you're not careful, you can lose sight of how precious they really are and just what God intends for them to become.

Raising children is more than just feeding and clothing them for eighteen years. It's more than just paying for their education and teaching them to drive. It's more than just keeping them out of the traffic and from falling down the stairs.

Raising our children should be an investment of our time, our wisdom, our experience, and a sharing of our love and ourselves. It should be a legacy, a passing on to

Ministry In Motherhood

the next generation, what we've learned and experienced and been blessed with.

Raising children can be the greatest blessing or the greatest heartbreak of your entire life. How it turns out in the end depends mostly on what you're willing to invest in it in the beginning, and all through those years when there is no end in sight.

Children are the most valuable treasures that God has entrusted to us. Inside the heart of every child is the potential to accomplish more for God than any one person has ever done before in history. What's more than that, inside the heart of every child also lies the faith to believe in something big that God could make of their lives, before the world has erased and reprogrammed their minds to fit in its mold.

Billy Sunday, D. L. Moody, John Wesley, George Washington, Abraham Lincoln, Florence Nightingale, Susannah Wesley, every Bible hero you can think of, every great man or woman living today that you can think of --- they were all children once. They all had big dreams and aspirations, and planned and pretended and play-acted about what they would someday become.

What is the difference between those who became great and those who never rose above the average, run-of-the-mill existence? Chances are, there was someone who made a difference in their lives, maybe even several someones. Someone who helped them believe in themselves. Someone who passed on wisdom and learning, who gave them direction and inspiration and encouragement to pursue their dreams. I would dare say that in many people's lives, that difference was made by a godly mother.

We've been given an awesome responsibility to train our children for the glory of God. Remember once again that God created mankind first of all to love Him, to spend time with Him and to glorify Him. As we train our children, we need to remember that is the primary purpose for their lives, as well as our own, and point them in that direction.

Psalm 127:3-4 says, *"Lo, children are an heritage of the LORD: and the fruit of the womb is his reward. As arrows are in the hand of a mighty man; so are children of the youth."* Children are a rich blessing and a valuable 'inheritance' that the Lord has placed in our possession.

As arrows are in the hand of a mighty man -- think about those words for a moment. David's soldiers were called his mighty men, and often in the Bible you'll find that term used to describe warriors who were greatly skilled in the use of their weapons. These were careful men, experienced men, men who had a target in sight, and knew how to take aim and to hit it.

Just as an arrow is in the hand of a man like this, God says that our children are placed in our hands for us to direct, to aim, to point toward the right target. The arrow, when placed in the hand of a skilled marksman, is a powerful weapon to withstand the attack of the enemy, and to secure victory in the battle.

How much more are our children a threat to the plans of the devil if we will be skillful as well as prayerful in directing their lives, and launching each of them toward a God-ordained goal in this spiritual warfare we're engaged in?

A spacecraft engineer pointed out the fact that a missile which is just a hairbreadth off target when it sits on the launching pad will be hundreds or even thousands of miles off when it reaches outer space. Then it's too late to correct the mistake.

How much better and easier will it be if we will examine and re-examine ourselves often during the years that we are raising our children, and try our very best to see that they are aimed in the right direction long before the time for 'lift-off'.

It's been said that, "Building children is better than mending adults." We have the blessed privilege and responsibility to carry out this task in the lives of the children that God has placed within our homes.

Prayer

The longer I live, and the older my children

become, the more I am convinced that the greatest thing I can do to love them, to protect them, to provide for them, to teach them, and to be what they need in a mother is to faithfully and fervently call out to God in their behalf.

It's scary to see them grow up and begin thinking their own thoughts and making their own plans. But God knows the number that rings their phone. Let's not wait until our children's lives are wrecked, when they're wandering in the world and far from God. Let's learn to pray for them daily, even hourly, while they're growing up in our homes.

Whether your child is learning to walk, learning to read, or learning to drive, he desperately needs your prayers. You can't see every trap that the devil has set in the path before him. You can't always identify every person who would influence your child to turn away from you and away from God. You don't always understand God's plans and purposes completely.

But God knows the beginning from the end, and hard as it is to imagine, He loves your children more than you do. Get in touch with Heaven, and become partners with the Lord in raising your children. There is no greater guarantee that we have to claim in behalf of our children than the promise that God hears and answers prayer.

There are many other areas we need to be reminded of as we endeavor to bring our children

Ministry In Motherhood

up in the nurture and admonition of the Lord, so I hope you'll join me as we continue this train of thought --- how to carry out the ministry that is ours in being mothers.

Raising Crops and Children

*I have seed to raise and I plow the field
And I plant my crops with care,
And I thank the Lord for the rain He sends,
As I watch them growing there.
But I don't sit down with a book by day
And let my crops run wild,
For crops won't prosper by themselves, I know;
Is it different with a child?*

*I've a boy to raise and I want a man
When his growing days are done;
And a man must work for the crop he seeks ---
Is it different with a son?
Will strangers care for my wheat out there
When the weeds grow rank and wild?
If my crop would shrink should I idle here,
Dare I idle with my child?*

*Yes, I'll work for him and I'll pray for him,
And I'll do the best I can,
For the Lord has given me a son to raise,
And I want to raise a man.
Yes, my eyes are set on the harvest years
When the long, hard task is done,
So I'll pull the weeds from his life, myself,
For I dare not shirk my son.*

---The Missouri Counsellor

Your Ministry in Motherhood - Continued

Chapter Seven

"...Take heed to the ministry which thou hast received in the Lord, that thou fulfil it."
(Colossians 4:17)

Have you ever paid close attention to what the Bible says about discipling converts? When we win a person to Christ, then we are responsible to see that they have the opportunity and the encouragement and teaching to follow through with baptism and then grow in the grace of God. *"Go ye therefore, and teach all nations, baptizing them in the name of the Father, and of the Son, and of the Holy Ghost: Teaching them to observe all things whatsoever I have commanded you:..."*

First we should teach them about salvation, then baptism, and then 'whatsoever I have commanded you.' Every command that has been given to me to obey as a child of God has also been given to my new convert, and it's my job to start teaching them these things, line upon line, a little bit at a time. "Whatsoever Jesus Has Commanded Me" is a large course of study, but it's also pretty well laid out for us, if we'll just stay in the Bible, and learn to apply Bible principles to our lives every day.

Paul said the same thing, that we are to pass on what we've learned to someone who will pass it on again. ***"And the things that thou hast heard of me among many witnesses, the same commit thou to faithful men, who shall be able to teach others also."*** (II Timothy 2:2) The most important converts of my whole Christian life are two little girls named Lydia and Rebekah Corle. The Lord gave me the privilege to lead them to Christ, and it's my job as their mother and as a Christian to teach them and to encourage them as much as any other convert.

I'm afraid we often see our responsibility to others without seeing our spiritual responsibility to those who call us 'Mom'. We have a bigger opportunity in discipling and training and teaching our children than any other person the Lord allows us to win to Christ. So what topics are included in 'whatsoever I have commanded you'?

Christian character is an important area. As the Lord has worked (and is working) in my heart to teach me and to make me what I ought to be, my children need to learn the same lessons. Kindness, courtesy, patience, thoughtfulness, generosity, dependability, responsibility, persistence, diligence, cheerfulness, purity; these are all things that I can point out, encourage, and expect in their lives.

Thousands of little lessons are much more effective than one big lesson. In our conversations, in our school work and home tasks, and in what I expect from their attitudes and actions, I can be helping them to form the kind of godly character traits that will please the Lord and help to prepare them for the Christian life.

Faithful service to the Lord is another area that I should be stressing. The Lord has already given us a built-in opportunity to be in full time service together as a family, and I value that a great deal. But I think it's important for every family to serve the Lord together in some area.

Maybe a bus route, maybe a junior church or some class, maybe a nursing home ministry, maybe a weekly soulwinning time -- the opportunities are endless. But I think it's important for our children to be able to see us in our service for Christ, and to have the chance to get involved and work along with us.

There is no greater training they can receive, and there is no better 'quality time' that we can spend with them. If all our family time is spent in recreation, I'm afraid our children get an artificial substitute for spending time with us and getting to know us. They need the chance to be with us in 'real life', too.

Ministry In Motherhood

What does the Lord want me to do for Him on a consistent basis? Prayer, Bible reading, soulwinning, faithful church attendance and involvement. These are a few of the things that ought to be tightly woven into the fabric of my life, and my children's lives, as well. I need to be stressing these godly habits and the reasons why they are so important, and helping my children incorporate them into the routine business of daily life.

Don't just send them soulwinning, take them and teach them how. Don't just say, "Read your Bible," but spend some time reading together, and also talking about how to read and study the Bible on their own.

Encourage them in their prayer lives, and make sure they know that you pray for them consistently, and pray together as a family. Pray about a test. Pray about a sick friend. Pray about a financial need. Just pray together about everything. We ought to be endeavoring to make these areas a real part of our daily lives.

You can only do so much, and then you have to get the Lord's help! I can remember a hot day in West Memphis, Arkansas when we were knocking on doors, and things didn't seem to be going very smooth. The girls were smaller at the time, and though they had won folks to Christ before, they were kind of hanging back and not wanting to talk to anyone that day.

The MRS. Ministry

I can remember praying silently (and somewhat desperately!), "Lord, You're the one who told me to teach them to do what You've commanded me to do, and I'm trying, but I'm not doing very well. I don't want my girls' memories of soulwinning to be like this. Please let them have something to get excited about in soulwinning today."

Within the next ten minutes, Lydia began talking to a man at the door, and won him to Christ. That was the first adult man she had ever won, and she went back to the truck yelling, "Daddy, I got one!"

I guess what I'm trying to say is this: no matter how hard I try, and how much I want to teach my children right, I still have to depend on the Lord and allow Him to work things out. I've seen the Lord do that time and time again in many different areas.

My children need to learn the Bible, and that's one area I want to concentrate on more in my family. I want them to be grounded in the Word; learning the stories, becoming familiar with the books of the Bible, their theme, the writers, and the history surrounding each one, memorizing God's Word and hiding it in their hearts.

Our children get a lot of preaching at church, and they have Bible as a subject in school, but I want to help it to become 'the engrafted

Word' that James speaks of, and literally become a part of their lives.

A very important part of their training at home is what they learn about the home and marriage and God-given romantic love, and how their teenage years and dating fit in with God's whole plan. It ought to be something that we talk about often, and in our family we do, but much more is 'caught' than 'taught'.

Living in a world where 'family' can mean any group of people living under the same roof in any kind of sinful situation, our children desperately need the background of a loving, stable relationship between their parents to help them form their own ideals and philosophies that will shape their family relationships someday.

One very special memory I have is a conversation my girls had with their dad earlier this year on the subject of purity and dating. It was thrilling for me to hear them voice some of the thoughts that they were thinking, and to see how much the Lord is working in their hearts and pointing out principles in the situations that they see. There is nothing more rewarding than to see and hear the proof of how the Holy Spirit is working in the hearts and lives of our children, and how they are responding and learning and growing.

I wish I could say that I think I'm doing well in ministering to my children. All I can really claim is that I want to do my best for them, and in my own feeble way, I'm trying.

The exciting part is that God is my partner in this endeavor, and He often fixes my boo-boos and succeeds where I feel I've failed. I'm talking to myself more than anyone else about what I think I ought to be teaching my children, and I hope I can make some improvements, too.

Remember our friend in Proverbs 31? She was truly in touch with her family. It says, *"She looketh well to the ways of her household..."* By household, I don't mean the laundry, cleaning, meals, and finances. I believe it means the people of the household, her family.

She looketh well to the ways of those people in her household. I should look well, keep a close watch, know their direction and what's on their mind, know what's important to them, their ups and downs. Looking well means a constant watchfulness over a constantly changing set of needs, and awareness of what they're going through, what they're learning, whether it's time to give them a hand of applause or a shoulder to cry on.

Our families need a 'mom' that cares enough to be involved and interested in their lives, and to look after each family member spiritually, as well as physically, working together as God's junior partner in raising our children to live for Him. *"Whereunto I also labour, striving*

Ministry In Motherhood

according to his working, which worketh in me mightily." (Colossians 1:29)

She's walking in my footsteps That's very plain to see -
She says that when she's grown up
She wants to be just like me.
But it's a scary feeling,
Though one that brings me pride,
And it makes me pause and ponder
My heart, and what's inside.

Do I really want her To be like me all the time?
Could I be proud to tell folks
That she's a child of mine?
Am I the kind of lady That I want my girls to be?
Would it make me happy
If they DID turn out like me?

Or would it bring me heartbreak
If those wishes did come true-
"Mommy when I'm grown up
I want to be just like you"?
Would I have to shed some tears
and bow my head in shame
If what I am today is what
my daughters soon became?

Dear Lord, I'm begging that You will
remind me everyday
That little girls are watching everything I do and say
Lord, make me the kind of lady
whose light the world can see
So I can be glad if my little girls
grow up to be just like me.

Cathy Corle 11-27-89

Our Ministry to The Membership and the Multitudes

Chapter Eight

"...Take heed to the ministry which thou hast received in the Lord, that thou fulfil it."
(Colossians 4:17)

It seems to me that I've fallen so far short in expressing the thoughts and ideas I started out wanting to share, but I hope that I've succeeded in getting this one idea across: your life is a ministry. My life is a ministry.

Every day that I live and breathe and function and enjoy life in the place where God has put me is my opportunity to give my life back to Him in love and worship and service. Being reminded that my life IS a ministry sure changes my perspective. It makes every situation and every relationship take on new meaning in my eyes.

Have you stopped to realize that your life is a ministry? Not just on Sunday, not just when you're at church, but you're in the ministry 24 hours a day, seven days a week. Every area of your daily life, every person that God has brought into your life, every job or responsibility that you face, presents you with your mission field.

We've talked about our ministry to our Maker. We've discussed many possibilities of ministering through our marriage. We've been reminded of some of the ways we can minister in our job as a mother.

Let me suggest just a few more ideas to you of areas where you have a ministry, an opportunity to meet needs, to serve and glorify the Lord, to draw people closer to Him.

Ministry to the Membership

In the local New Testament church where God has placed you, you have an opportunity -- in fact, many opportunities -- to carry out your ministry.

I don't know what positions you fill at your church. Maybe as a Sunday School teacher or Junior Church worker. Maybe as a bus captain. Maybe as a choir member or pianist or organist. Maybe you work in the nursery.

Be reminded and encouraged about the opportunities that already lie at your feet. These are avenues through which you can touch lives and share the love of God with others. These are ways in which you can uplift and glorify God and seek to introduce others to Him and to draw them closer to Him.

Many ladies already have more than enough opportunity to serve the Lord in their local church, but maybe you have allowed it to become stale and meaningless. Perhaps you've lost sight of the glorious privilege that is ours to be an active part of a church that is publishing the Good News, and reaching out with the Gospel.

Take a minute to close your eyes and picture those young faces from your Sunday School class as they listen to you teach from the Word of God. Let yourself be reminded of the homes they come from, and the pressures and heartaches they face. Think about the privilege that you have to stand before them each week and try to direct their attention to God and His Word and to be a major influence in their lives. If we take the time to pause and love them in our hearts for a while, no one will have to hound us to visit them, pray for them, or take an active interest in their lives.

If you're in the bus ministry, you have a grand opportunity to reach into the homes of boys and girls who will never be taken to church, never hear a Bible story, and even some who will never be loved and cared for unless you care enough to do so. Stop and allow yourself to realize that all over again.

All the reasons that caused you to want to become involved in this ministry in the first place

Ministry to the Membership & Multitudes

are the reasons that should motivate and inspire you to keep on.

What about the nursery? In some churches, this can become a sore spot. "Do I have to be in the nursery again? Isn't it somebody else's turn?" Those who say those things (whether silently or aloud) have not stopped to realize how important their ministry is.

When my children were babies, they were in different nurseries every week. Believe me, we've seen the best and the worst, the cleanest and the dirtiest, the most caring and the most careless.

There were times when I absolutely could not pay attention to the message because my mind was wondering whether my baby would still be alive and well when I got back to her. I would shake my head and wonder, "If it's that hard for me to put my baby in their nursery, how in the world can they expect unsaved people to come in and feel comfortable, and think they can enjoy the service and hear the sermon enough to respond to it and then want to come back again?"

On the flip side, I often got to take my babies to a nursery where I was met at the door by a smiling face, and someone who made me feel that my child was in the best of care. Their clean, well cared-for facilities, and careful, thoughtful procedures helped me to feel at ease about my child and to be able to concentrate on the service.

The MRS. Ministry

I'm convinced that the church nursery is a much more important ministry than most of its workers consider it to be.

When you work in the nursery, you're helping to win souls, because you're making it possible for visitors to come to the service and hear the Gospel uninterrupted and undistracted. When you do your best to have a top notch ministry in the nursery, you're making it easier for visitors with babies to come to church the first time, and you're multiplying the likelihood of those newly saved converts coming to church consistently enough to grow in grace and become faithful church members.

By working in the nursery, you are helping the pastor as he preaches, because you are removing many of the disruptions that would come up in the service and make it difficult for him to communicate a message and hold the attention of the crowd. You have a very important part, and it is vital that you excel at your job in the nursery. This is an important avenue of ministry.

The opportunities are endless. Junior church. A girl's club, like Proverbs 31 or Blue Denim and Lace. Cleaning the church. Organizing meals for funerals and illnesses. Sending out birthday cards, handling the Sunday School records -- there are so many ways in which you could be a blessing and an important part of the ministry at your church.

Ministry to the Membership & Multitudes

Maybe you haven't yet become involved in the ministry of your church, and the Lord has been speaking to your heart about it. How do the needs and the unfilled jobs at your church match up with the abilities that you have and the burden that God has placed on your heart for a certain area?

Don't let the devil continue to talk you out of it, and don't let him keep telling you that you're unqualified and unwanted. (I know that's what he's been telling you, because that's what he tells all of us.) Check with your preacher about where there's a need that you could fill. Make yourself available. Be cooperative. Be diligent. Be supportive of the pastor. You can be a great blessing in your local church.

I've mentioned a few of the ways that you can be a part of the organized ministry at your local church, but you have many more opportunities of ministry to your church family. Remember that lady whose husband left her and she's not sure how she's going to make it through the next week? You could give her a call or send her a card that says, "I'm praying for you." You could stop by with a batch of cookies and drink a cup of coffee with her to let her know that you care about her loneliness and pain.

Maybe someone has lost a loved one or has a family member in the hospital. You could fix a meal, or offer to run errands or do the grocery

The MRS. Ministry

shopping or the laundry. Sometimes the smallest things that we do in a time of need carry the biggest message that says, "I care."

Your church is full of people that you can minister to when they have a need, and every one of them will have those needs at some time or another. You have an opportunity to love, encourage, exhort, and be there for someone who is in need.

Don't forget about your pastor and his family. I sometimes see churches where the members 'spoil' the preacher and his family, and that is wonderful. But it grieves my heart when I see a man and his wife and family who are giving of themselves and carrying the load and the people of the church don't seem to appreciate it or notice it at all.

Now I know that they are not doing it for the church's appreciation or applause, and I trust that they'll keep on serving the Lord faithfully no matter what the rest of the church does. But it sure would be encouraging to them if they got a note that says, "I think you are the greatest preacher and preacher's wife in the world, and I'm so glad God brought you to our city and our church."

It would mean a lot to the preacher and his wife and children if you did something thoughtful for them, or volunteered to help lift the load when they are extra busy. You have no idea how important your ministry to them might be.

Ministry to the Multitudes

Finally, let's not forget the ministry that we have to the whole world -- the opportunity and obligation to give the Gospel to every creature. What a blessing it is to sit down with someone who says, "No, I'm not sure of Heaven when I die," and have such wonderful news to share with them from the Word of God.

I trust that you're a part of a soulwinning church that has regular, scheduled times to go door-to-door and meet people, looking for that one who is ready to be saved. There are many more opportunities in our daily lives that we miss simply because we're not looking for them.

Remember what it's like to have good news to share? You can't even wait for someone to get inside the house, but you have to rush out and meet them in the driveway and yell out the reason for your happiness.

There has never been any greater news in the world than, *"But God commendeth his love toward us, in that, while we were yet sinners, Christ died for us."* Or, *"For God so loved the world that he gave his only begotten Son, that whosoever believeth in him should not perish, but have everlasting life."* It's fun to get to be the one who spills out the good news, but with most good news, we don't have the devil fighting against us and trying to steal our joy and our fervor. We don't have anyone whispering, "They'll just get mad and slam the door on you," or "You'll forget what you were going to say and make an idiot of yourself."

The devil can't take away our Good News, and he can't keep lost people from hearing it and receiving it and rejoicing in it. So he spends his time and energy trying to discourage us and distract us from our exciting job of sharing God's good news.

We have a ministry to the multitudes in sharing a verbal message, and we also have the responsibility to share a visible message. We get to represent God to the unsaved, to be an ambassador of the kingdom of heaven in this old world.

Our lives ought to point out the fact that we belong to the Lord, and our testimonies ought to remind folks to Whom we belong. There should be some 'family resemblance' that folks can see in us the love and the character of our heavenly Father. We can be the 'salt of the earth' that makes people thirsty for a taste of the Water of Life, the Lord Jesus Christ.

We have a ministry that includes every person we pass everyday, a ministry to the multitudes. We are entrusted with the Gospel message, the Good News that Jesus Christ died on

Ministry to the Membership & Multitudes

the cross, was buried and rose again so that He could take our sin debt upon Himself and purchase with His own blood our pardon, our peace and our place in Heaven. It's a ministry of reconciliation Paul said, reconciling sinful man with a Holy God.

How have we been doing in this ministry?

*Christ has no hands but our hands to do His work today --
He has no feet but our feet to lead men in His way.
He has no tongue but our tongue to tell them how He died,
He has no help but our help to bring them to His side.*

*We are the only Bible the careless world will read
We are the sinner's Gospel -- We are the scoffer's creed.
We are the Lord's last message given in deed and word;
What if the type is crooked? What if the print is blurred?*

*What if our hands are busy with other work than His?
What if our feet are walking where sin's allurement is?
What if our tongues are speaking of things His lips would spurn?
How can we hope to help Him, and hasten His return. (copied)*

So, tell me about your ministry. Who are the people that God has placed in your life to minister to and meet needs for? What are the opportunities that you have to serve the Lord in your home and in your church? Who has the Lord placed in your path so that you can have a part in helping them to draw closer to the Lord? These are the avenues of ministry that the Lord has opened up to you.

I'm sure this won't be the last time that you

The MRS. Ministry

and I need to be reminded that our lives are a ministry of service to God and for God. But I hope that its an effective and productive reminder, even though it won't be the last one.

This Bible exhortation is for us: *"...Take heed to the ministry which thou hast received in the Lord, that thou fulfil it."* (Colossians 4:17)

IF YOU WERE TO DIE TODAY, ARE YOU 100% SURE THAT YOU WOULD GO TO HEAVEN?

If you could know that, you would want to, wouldn't you?

"Wherefore, as by one man sin entered into the world, and death by sin: and so death passed upon all men, for that all have sinned:" (Romans 5:12) The one thing that stands between us and going to Heaven when we die is our sin --- and God said that ALL have sinned. He didn't leave anyone out. If I'm going to be honest with myself, I must admit that I am included.

I am a sinner first of all because I inherited a sinful nature from Adam that has been passed down to me. I am a sinner because I have disobeyed the clear commands of God. Just as it only takes one instance of stealing to make me a thief, it takes only one sin to make me a sinner.

There are no 'good sinners' or 'bad sinners' in the eyes of God --- we all stand guilty before

Him, and unworthy of Heaven.

The Bible says that there is a penalty for sin --- DEATH. *"...and so death passed upon all men, for that all have sinned." (Romans 5:12) "for the wages of sin is death..." (Romans 6:23)* You cannot pay for sin by going to church or being baptized or doing good deeds or keeping commandments. The only payment that will clear your account is death. This is not just a physical death. The Bible is clear that after the body dies, there is a second death or a spiritual death.

"But the fearful, and unbelieving, and the abominable, and murderers, and whoremongers, and sorcerers, and idolaters, and all liars, shall have their part in the lake which burneth with fire and brimstone which is the second death." (Revelation 21:8) The Bible is clear that if we must pay the price for our own sin, we must suffer a second death forever in the lake of fire called hell. No other payment that we can make would pay the price, because the wages of sin is death.

God loves us so much that He did not want us to go to hell, even though we deserve to do so. Yet he would not be just and righteous if He allowed us to go to Heaven with our sin, just as a judge would be unjust to let a murderer go free just because it was someone he knew and loved.

Sin must be paid for. There is only one way for our sin to be paid for without you and me spending all eternity in the torment of Hell: that is to let Someone else pay the price for us.

"For God so loved the world, that he gave his only begotten Son, that whosoever believeth

in him should not perish, but have everlasting life." (John 3:16) God allowed His Son, Jesus Christ, to suffer and die in our place to pay the price of death that we owe. We do not need to do anything to earn it, we must simply receive the salvation that Jesus paid for with His blood.

"*But as many as received him, to them gave he power to become the sons of God, even to them that believe on his name:*" (John 1:12) If we will receive Jesus and His death on the cross as payment for our sins, He has promised to receive us into His family as a child of God.

"*Behold, I stand at the door, and knock: if any man hear my voice, and open the door, I will come in to him...*" (Revelation 3:20) Receiving Christ is as simple as opening the door and inviting someone in. Christ stands ready to come into your heart, forgive your sins, and make you a child of God. But he will only come by invitation. Won't you bow your head right now, wherever you are, and invite the Lord Jesus Christ to come in?

Lord Jesus,
I know that I am a sinner, and that I deserve to go to hell. Please forgive me and come into my heart right now. I'm trusting you to make me a child of God, to take me to Heaven when I die, and to help me live the rest of my life for you. Thank you for saving me. In Jesus' name, Amen

If you sincerely prayed that prayer and asked the Lord to save you, He said, "*...I will* *come in."* That's not a maybe. He promised that He would. If you died right now with Christ in your heart where would you go? To Heaven! If you had died before you asked Christ into your heart, where would you have gone? The difference between heaven and hell is the Lord Jesus Christ living within, Who died to pay the price of our sin.

Now that Christ lives in your heart, He has promised that He will never leave. *"...for he hath said, I will never leave thee, nor forsake thee."* No matter when you die, Christ will still be in your heart as He promised, so Heaven is as sure as if you were already there.

God does expect us to obey Him after we become His children, and the very first command that He gives is found in Acts 2:38. *"...Repent, and be baptized every one of you..."* Repentance takes place within, when I turn away from sin and self and turn to Christ as my Savior. Baptism is the outward sign of what has happened in my heart --- a picture of the death, burial and resurrection of Jesus. Immediately after we get saved, God expects us to be baptized and show the world that we belong to Him.

If you have received Christ into your heart as a result of reading this book, please write and let us know. We'd like to send you a free copy of GROWING UP IN GOD'S FAMILY and LIVING UP TO YOUR NAME.

_____
Name

_____
Address

_____
City, State, Zip

_____
Phone Number

Send to:
Dennis Corle Evangelistic Assoc.
Revival Fires!
P.O. Box 245 • Claysburg, PA 16625
(814) 239-2813